EARLY PHYSICS FUN
TRAMPOLINES

by Jenny Fretland VanVoorst

pogo

Ideas for Parents and Teachers

Pogo Books let children practice reading informational text while introducing them to nonfiction features such as headings, labels, sidebars, maps, and diagrams, as well as a table of contents, glossary, and index.

Carefully leveled text with a strong photo match offers early fluent readers the support they need to succeed.

Before Reading

- "Walk" through the book and point out the various nonfiction features. Ask the student what purpose each feature serves.
- Look at the glossary together. Read and discuss the words.

Read the Book

- Have the child read the book independently.
- Invite him or her to list questions that arise from reading.

After Reading

- Discuss the child's questions. Talk about how he or she might find answers to those questions.
- Prompt the child to think more. Ask: Have you ever jumped on a trampoline? Did you know that trampoline is now an Olympic event? You can watch videos of competitions online.

To Rosita, Lily, and Luke, with thanks.

Pogo Books are published by Jump!
5357 Penn Avenue South
Minneapolis, MN 55419
www.jumplibrary.com

Library of Congress Cataloging-in-Publication Data

Names: Fretland VanVoorst, Jenny, 1972- author.
Title: Trampolines / by Jenny Fretland VanVoorst.
Description: Minneapolis, MN: Jump!, Inc. [2016] |
Series: Early physics fun | Audience: Ages 7-10. |
Includes index.
Identifiers: LCCN 2015039670| ISBN 9781620313190
(hardcover: alk. paper) | ISBN 9781624963711 (ebook)
Subjects: LCSH: Trampolines–Juvenile literature. | Force and energy–Juvenile literature. | Physics–Study and teaching (Elementary)–Juvenile literature.
Classification: LCC GV555.F74 2016 | DDC 531.6–dc23
LC record available at http://lccn.loc.gov/2015039670

Series Designer: Anna Peterson
Photo Researcher: Anna Peterson

Photo Credits: All photos by Shutterstock except:
Alamy, 1; Domini Brown, 12, 13, 14-15, 16-17;
Getty, 20-21; Nicku/Shutterstock.com, 28;
SuperStock, 10-11; Thinkstock, 4, 19.

Printed in the United States of America at Corporate Graphics in North Mankato, Minnesota.

TABLE OF CONTENTS

CHAPTER 1

ENERGY

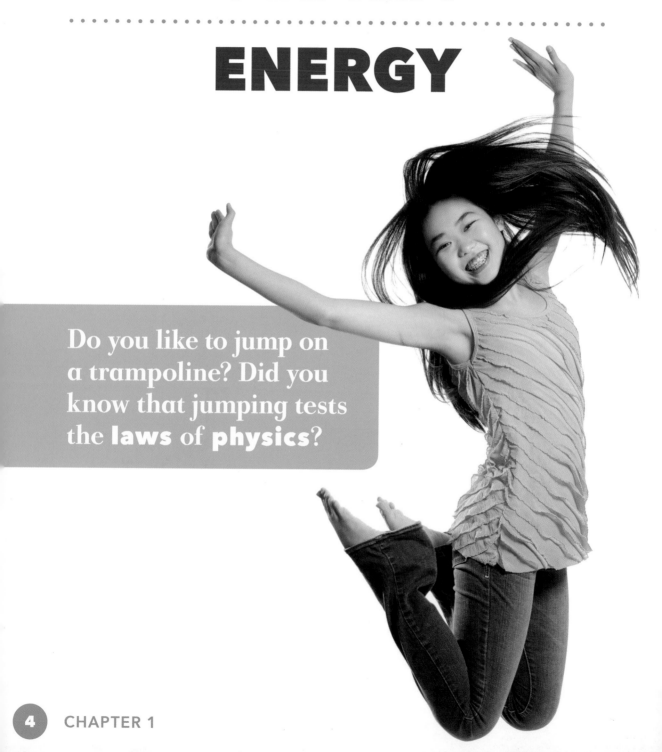

Do you like to jump on a trampoline? Did you know that jumping tests the **laws** of **physics**?

Physics is the science of matter and how it moves. There are physics laws by which all things work.

A trampoline is just a mat fixed to a frame by springs. And yet it works based on several physics laws.

DID YOU KNOW?

Be safe! Before you jump, check your equipment. Make sure it is in good shape. Check that there is enough padding. Have an adult on hand. And jump one at a time.

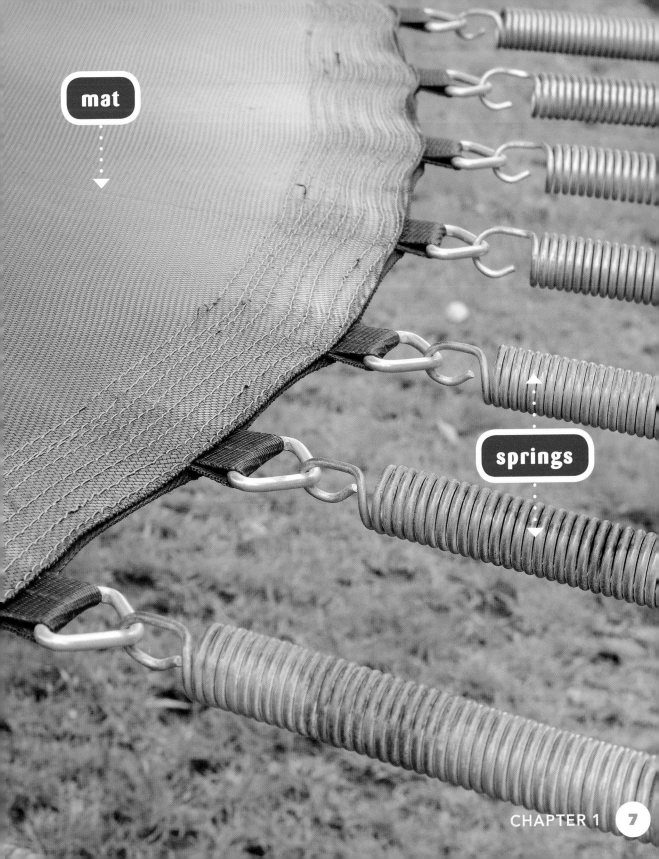

mat

springs

Jumping uses energy.
But what kind?

Kinetic energy is the fun energy. It is the energy of being in motion. It increases with speed. It decreases when you slow down.

Potential energy is the energy a thing has as a result of its location. It is stored energy.

Jumping on a trampoline uses both kinds of energy. How?

As you rise, you slow down. Kinetic energy turns into potential energy. The higher you are, the more potential energy you have. As you fall, you speed up. Potential energy becomes kinetic energy.

TAKE A LOOK!

Stored energy is greatest at the highest point of your jump. Energy from motion is highest just before you bounce.

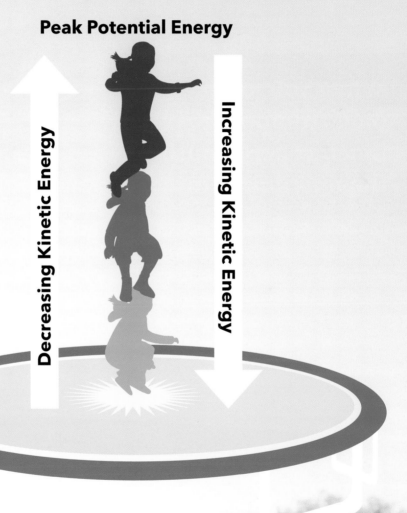

Peak Potential Energy

Decreasing Kinetic Energy

Increasing Kinetic Energy

CHAPTER 2

HOOKE'S LAW

When you jump on a trampoline, kinetic energy pushes the mat downward.

This stretches the springs. Then what happens?

Hooke's Law states that stretched springs will work to return to their original state. They will resist being stretched.

So as the springs **contract**, they pull the mat with them. The mat returns to its original position. You are shot up into the air!

TAKE A LOOK!

When weight is applied, springs stretch. When the weight is removed, they return to their original state.

2 LBS (1.4 KG)

4 LBS (2.8 KG)

6 LBS (4.2 KG)

Original State

CHAPTER 3

NEWTON'S THIRD LAW

Newton's Third Law of Motion is one of the most famous laws of physics.

Sir Isaac Newton

This law states that for every action there is an equal and opposite reaction. What does this have to do with trampolines?

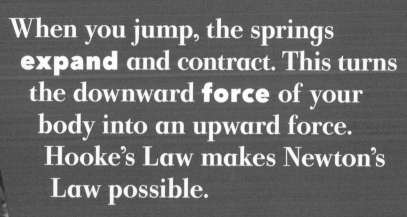

When you jump, the springs **expand** and contract. This turns the downward **force** of your body into an upward force. Hooke's Law makes Newton's Law possible.

These laws make trampolines fun. And that means fun for you!

DID YOU KNOW?

Sir Isaac Newton was an English scientist. He made many important discoveries. He had two other laws of motion. Look them up!

ACTIVITIES & TOOLS

DOES BIGGER MEAN BOUNCIER?

Does weight affect how high you can bounce? Let's find out. You'll need access to a trampoline for this activity.

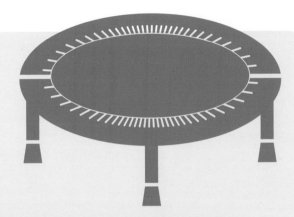

1. First, you'll need to collect data. Start by jumping on the trampoline yourself. Find a way to measure how high you jump. Maybe have somebody hold a yardstick above the trampoline and then record how high your feet get off the mat.

2. Then have a smaller child jump, and then an adult. Measure the heights they reach.

3. Now it's time to look at your findings. Was there a difference in how high each person got off the trampoline?

4. Finally, think about your findings. Do you think the differences in jump height had to do with weight or something else, like how muscular each person was and how much force he or she jumped with?

contract: To draw or squeeze together so as to make or become smaller or shorter and broader.

expand: To grow larger or wider as a result of being released from pressure.

force: An influence (as a push or pull) that tends to produce a change in the speed or direction of motion of something.

Hooke's Law: A physics law that states that a stretched spring wants to return to its natural, unstretched state.

kinetic energy: Energy associated with motion.

law: A basic rule or principle.

Newton's Third Law of Motion: A physics law that states that for every action there is an equal and opposite reaction.

physics: The science that involves the study of matter and how it moves through space and time; it includes concepts such as energy and force.

potential energy: Energy associated with location.

INDEX

TO LEARN MORE

Learning more is as easy as 1, 2, 3.

1) Go to www.factsurfer.com

2) Enter "trampolines" into the search box.

3) Click the "Surf" button to see a list of websites.

With factsurfer, finding more information is just a click away.